DATE DUE

NOV 3 0 1999			
MAR 1 6 2001			
MAY 2 9 2012			
MAR 1 9 2015			
APR 0 7 2015			
5/29/15			

Demco, Inc. 38-293

Serial Murder

CRIME, JUSTICE, AND PUNISHMENT

Serial Murder

HPHS IMC

Robert W. Dolan

Austin Sarat, GENERAL EDITOR

CHELSEA HOUSE PUBLISHERS
Philadelphia

Frontispiece: Looking for clues in a serial murder case.

Chelsea House Publishers

Production Manager Pamela Loos
Art Director Sara Davis
Picture Editor Judy Hasday
Senior Production Editor Lisa Chippendale

Staff for SERIAL MURDER

Senior Editor John Ziff
Designer Takeshi Takahashi
Picture Researcher Gillian Speeth
Cover Illustration Janet Hamlin

3 5 7 9 8 6 4 2

Library of Congress Cataloging-in-Publication Data

Dolan, Robert W.
Serial murder / Robert W. Dolan ; Austin Sarat, general editor.
    p. cm. — (Crime, justice, and punishment)
Includes bibliographical references and index.
Summary: Examines the psychology of the serial killer and the challenges such criminals present to law enforcement personnel.

ISBN 0-7910-4275-8

1. Serial murder investigation—Juvenile literature. 2. Serial murders—History—Juvenile literature. 3. Serial murderers—Psychology—Juvenile literature. [1. Murder.] I. Sarat, Austin. II. Title. III. Series.
HV8079.H6D65 1997
364.15'23—dc21   97-8598
                                              CIP
                                              AC

Contents

CRIME, JUSTICE, AND PUNISHMENT

CAPITAL PUNISHMENT

CLASSIC CONS AND SWINDLES

DETECTIVES, PRIVATE EYES,
AND BOUNTY HUNTERS

THE FBI'S MOST WANTED

HATE CRIMES

INFAMOUS TRIALS

THE JURY

JUVENILE CRIME

PRISONS

RACE AND CRIME

REVENGE AND RETRIBUTION

RIGHTS OF THE ACCUSED

SERIAL MURDER

TERRORISM

VICTIMS AND VICTIMS' RIGHTS

WHITE-COLLAR CRIME

Fears and Fascinations:

An Introduction to Crime, Justice, and Punishment

By Austin Sarat

e live with crime and images of crime all around us. Crime evokes in most of us a deep aversion, a feeling of profound vulnerability, but it also evokes an equally deep fascination. Today, in major American cities the fear of crime is a major fact of life, some would say a disproportionate response to the realities of crime. Yet the fear of crime is real, palpable in the quickened steps and furtive glances of people walking down darkened streets. At the same time, we eagerly follow crime stories on television and in movies. We watch with a "who done it" curiosity, eager to see the illicit deed done, the investigation undertaken, the miscreant brought to justice and given his just deserts. On the streets the presence of crime is a reminder of our own vulnerability and the precariousness of our taken-for-granted rights and freedoms. On television and in the movies the crime story gives us a chance to probe our own darker motives, to ask "Is there a criminal within?" as well as to feel the collective satisfaction of seeing justice done.

Fear and fascination, these two poles of our engagement with crime, are, of course, only part of the story. Crime is, after all, a major social and legal problem, not just an issue of our individual psychology. Politicians today use our fear of, and fascination with, crime for political advantage. How we respond to crime, as well as to the political uses of the crime issue, tells us a lot about who we are as a people as well as what we value and what we tolerate. Is our response compassionate or severe? Do we seek to understand or to punish, to enact an angry vengeance or to rehabilitate and welcome the criminal back into our midst? The CRIME, JUSTICE, AND PUNISHMENT series is designed to explore these themes, to ask why we are fearful and fascinated, to probe the meanings and motivations of crimes and criminals and of our responses to them, and, finally, to ask what we can learn about ourselves and the society in which we live by examining our responses to crime.

Crime is always a challenge to the prevailing normative order and a test of the values and commitments of law-abiding people. It is sometimes a Raskolnikov-like act of defiance, an assertion of the unwillingness of some to live according to the rules of conduct laid out by organized society. In this sense, crime marks the limits of the law and reminds us of law's all-too-regular failures. Yet sometimes there is more desperation than defiance in criminal acts; sometimes they signal a deep pathology or need in the criminal. To confront crime is thus also to come face-to-face with the reality of social difference, of class privilege and extreme deprivation, of race and racism, of children neglected, abandoned, or abused whose response is to enact on others what they have experienced themselves. And occasionally crime, or what is labeled a criminal act, represents a call for justice, an appeal to a higher moral order against the inadequacies of existing law.

Figuring out the meaning of crime and the motivations of criminals and whether crime arises from defiance, desperation, or the appeal for justice is never an easy task. The motivations and meanings of crime are as varied as are the persons who engage in criminal conduct. They are as mysterious as any of the mysteries of the human soul. Yet the desire to know the secrets of crime and the criminal is a strong one, for in that knowledge may lie one step on the road to protection, if not an assurance of one's own personal safety. Nonetheless, as strong as that desire may be, there is no available technology that can allow us to know the whys of crime with much confidence, let alone a scientific certainty. We can, however, capture something about crime by studying the defiance, desperation, and quest for justice that may be associated with it. Books in the CRIME, JUSTICE, AND PUNISHMENT series will take up that challenge. They tell stories of crime and criminals, some famous, most not, some glamorous and exciting, most mundane and commonplace.

This series will, in addition, take a sober look at American criminal justice, at the procedures through which we investigate crimes and identify criminals, at the institutions in which innocence or guilt is determined. In these procedures and institutions we confront the thrill of the chase as well as the challenge of protecting the rights of those who defy our laws. It is through the efficiency and dedication of law enforcement that we might capture the criminal; it is in the rare instances of their corruption or brutality that we feel perhaps our deepest betrayal. Police, prosecutors, defense lawyers, judges, and jurors administer criminal justice and in their daily actions give substance to the guarantees of the Bill of Rights. What is an adversarial system of justice? How does it work? Why do we have it? Books in the CRIME, JUSTICE, AND PUNISHMENT series will examine the thrill of the chase as we seek to capture the criminal. They will also reveal the drama and majesty of the criminal trial as well as the day-to-day reality of a criminal justice system in which trials are the exception and negotiated pleas of guilty are the rule.

When the trial is over or the plea has been entered, when we have separated the innocent from the guilty, the moment of punishment has arrived. The injunction to punish the guilty, to respond to pain inflicted by inflicting pain, is as old as civilization itself. "An eye for an eye and a tooth for a tooth" is a biblical reminder that punishment must measure pain for pain. But our response to the criminal must be better than and different from the crime itself. The biblical admonition, along with the constitutional prohibition of "cruel and unusual punishment," signals that we seek to punish justly and to be just not only in the determination of who can and should be punished, but in how we punish as well. But neither reminder tells us what to do with the wrongdoer. Do we rape the rapist, or burn the home of the arsonist? Surely justice and decency say no. But, if not, then how can and should we punish? In a world in which punishment is neither identical to the crime nor an automatic response to it, choices must be made and we must make them. Books in the CRIME, JUSTICE, AND PUNISHMENT series will examine those choices and the practices, and politics, of punishment. How do we punish and why do we punish as we do? What can we learn about the rationality and appropriateness of today's responses to crime by examining our past and its responses? What works? Is there, and can there be, a just measure of pain?

CRIME, JUSTICE, AND PUNISHMENT brings together books on some of the great themes of human social life. The books in this series capture our fear and fascination with crime and examine our responses to it. They remind us of the deadly seriousness of these subjects. They bring together themes in law, literature, and popular culture to challenge us to think again, to think anew, about subjects that go to the heart of who we are and how we can and will live together.

* * * * *

The unjustified taking of the life of another human being—murder—is in itself almost unimaginably horrible. While this horror happens with alarming frequency throughout the United States, we are still left with the difficult task of trying to understand murder and murderers. Who are they? Why do they do what they do? This task is all the more difficult when the murderer kills many people, over an extended period of time, when he tortures or dehumanizes his victims, and when, during the reign of terror that serial killing brings, he lives what seems to be an otherwise normal life.

Serial Murder provides a vivid and compelling account of the crime and the criminals who commit it. Drawing on in-depth case studies of serial killers, this book helps us understand who they are and why they do what they do. It helps us see the deep and persistent pathologies that give rise to the impulse to murder and to ritualize and take pleasure in the crime. It reminds us of both the stark horror of this crime and the fact that the incidence of serial murder is on the rise. It provides an insightful look at the challenges that serial murder poses for law enforcement and at the way police go about profiling the serial killer and investigating his crimes. In the end this book correctly warns us that there are no quick fixes or sure cures for this social menace.

MURDERERS
AMONG US

In 1960 a knife-wielding madman dressed in the clothes of his dead mother attacked a beautiful woman in a shower and forever altered the face of horror in America. The murder occurred in Alfred Hitchcock's *Psycho*, a movie that not only changed the way an entire generation felt about being alone in the bathroom but also gave birth to a new kind of bogeyman. *Psycho*'s monster was not a vampire or a hideous creature from outer space but a shy, quiet, stuttering bachelor with a friendly smile, a simple personality, and the very ordinary name of Norman Bates.

Psycho frightens us because it transforms the familiar sights of the everyday world into something unspeakably horrible. Before we know it, we are in a place where a motel bathroom becomes a chamber of horrors; where an easygoing, perfectly harmless man changes into a crazed, knife-carrying transvestite; and where a helpless old lady turns out to be a long-dead corpse dressed in a scarf and wig. When the movie is

13

over, we feel as if we have just awakened from an awful nightmare, thankful that the movie was only fiction.

Of all the terrors associated with *Psycho,* the greatest terror is this: it is based on the truth. There really was a Norman Bates.

His name wasn't Norman, and he didn't run a motel. But on a secluded farm in Plainfield, Wisconsin, during the 1950s, there lived a shy, single man with a friendly smile and a quiet personality. His neighbors knew him as a slightly odd but easygoing fellow, the kind of man they could count on to help out with any chore that needed to be done. Little did they know, he was also a robber of graves, a butcher of women, a transvestite who dressed himself not in the clothes but in the very skin of his female victims.

For years his gruesome deeds went undetected. When he was finally brought to justice, the details of his crimes shocked and horrified the nation. A writer named Robert Bloch used the story as the basis for his novel *Psycho,* which in turn was the basis for Hitchcock's film. The crimes also inspired at least two other movies, the 1974 cult hit *The Texas Chainsaw Massacre* and the 1991 Academy Award winner *The Silence of the Lambs.* The name of the real-life Norman Bates was Edward Gein (pronounced with a long *e,* as in *fiend*). He was the cinema's most influential serial killer.

In recent years, serial killers have figured prominently on the small screen as well. Scores of made-for-TV movies and police series focusing on serial murder have been aired, and viewers have become familiar—at least insofar as the television versions present an accurate picture—with a kind of criminal whose existence was virtually unknown little more than a generation ago.

In addition to the TV and movie depictions, Americans have learned about the cases of real-life serial killers from the print media's abundant coverage. Since the late 1970s a succession of chilling figures have

seized headlines and horrified the public: Ted Bundy; David Berkowitz, New York City's "Son of Sam"; John Wayne Gacy; Richard Ramirez, "the Night Stalker" of Los Angeles; Jeffrey Dahmer.

All of this recent attention might lead a casual observer to conclude that serial murder is a recent phenomenon, and indeed, there are sources that describe it as such. For example, Eric van Hoffmann, author of *A Venom in the Blood*, dates the appearance of serial killers to the year 1972, and the term *serial murder* was coined in the early 1970s. But recent recognition and new

Ed Gein (center) on his way to jail. A serial murderer who dressed in the skin of his victims, Gein inspired the motion pictures Psycho, The Texas Chainsaw Massacre, *and* The Silence of the Lambs.

terminology don't necessarily mean a new problem. Criminologist James Reinhardt discussed the subject of "chain killers" as early as 1962, and the problem was already ancient. Serial murder may, in fact, be as old as human history.

In 5th-century Aden, a port city on the southern part of the Arabian Peninsula, a wealthy man by the name of Zu Shenatir lured young boys to his home with offers of food and money. He would rape them before tossing them out an upstairs window to their deaths. Zu Shenatir's body count is unknown, but history tells us that he was stabbed to death at his home by a would-be victim.

In Europe, serial killers came from the rich and the poor of society alike. Gilles de Rais, the wealthiest man in France, friend and advisor to Joan of Arc, was executed in 1440 for killing more than 100 children. In 1611 a Hungarian countess named Elisabeth Bathory was convicted of killing some 650 young women for the purpose of bathing in their blood. In 1719 Italian authorities executed another female killer, La Tofania, for poisoning 600 victims. Joseph Phillipe butchered French prostitutes in the 1860s, and Jack the Ripper followed in his footsteps, slaughtering five prostitutes in the Whitechapel section of London in 1888 and, in the process, becoming one of the most infamous serial killers of all time.

In the United States, a sadist by the name of Herman Mudgett built a custom-made "murder castle" in Chicago to dispose of women during the 1893 World's Fair. He was convicted of only a single murder, but Mudgett confessed to 26 others before he was hanged. More recently, Cleveland's "Mad Butcher" dissected 16 victims in the 1930s, outsmarting famed crime fighter Eliot Ness. The killings became known as the "Torso Slayings," and the killer was never caught.

If serial murder isn't new, it does seem to be becoming more common. Since 1960, not only has the number of known serial killers increased, but so has the number of victims per killer. The Federal Bureau of Investigation (FBI) has estimated that there are at least 500 serial killers at large and unidentified in this country. Among them are the Green River Killer of the Seattle, Washington, area, who claimed as many as 49 female victims between July 1982 and March 1984; the Frankford Stalker, who beat and stabbed to death nine female residents of Philadelphia between 1985 and

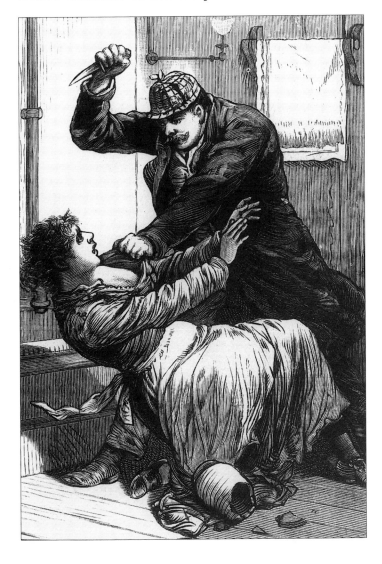

This 1889 woodcut from the Police Gazette depicts the artist's conception of an attack by Jack the Ripper, killer of five London prostitutes, whom experts consider the first modern serial murderer. The Ripper's identity has never been definitively established, nor is it known precisely how he committed his crimes.

1990; and New York City's ".22-caliber gunman," blamed for the murders of seven taxi drivers in 1990. In addition, police continue to investigate a string of prostitute murders in Los Angeles and a series of slayings of homeless men in San Francisco and other cities, in which the victims have been found with the sign of the pentagram carved into their flesh.

The perpetrators of these crimes belong to a class of murderers who don't know their victims but kill for the sheer "high" of the experience. The FBI calls these homicides *serial murders* and the killers *recreational* or *lust* killers.

In any discussion of serial murder, settling upon a definition can be problematic. Self-proclaimed experts argue endlessly about the body count or the length of time between each crime that is required for a murderer to be a "genuine" serial killer. The FBI's Behavioral Science Unit defines serial murder as "three or more separate events with an emotional cooling-off period between homicides," with each murder taking place at a different location. As straightforward as this may seem, the FBI's definition has problems, the largest of which is its failure to determine the "cooling-off period" between homicides. And the FBI definition fails to account for serial killers like John Wayne Gacy, who murdered more than one victim at the same location. In 1988 the federally funded National Institute of Justice defined serial murder as

> a series of two or more murders, committed as separate events, usually, but not always, by one offender acting alone. The crimes may occur over a period of time ranging from hours to years. Quite often the motive is psychological, and the offender's behavior and the physical evidence observed at the crime scenes will reflect sadistic, sexual overtones.

Using these criteria, the criminologist Michael Newton has identified 835 cases of serial murder since 1900, involving some 1,008 individual killers and an estimated 7,195 to 9,401 victims. The exact number of killers remains uncertain because of unsolved cases and may be considerably higher.

Some authorities believe that almost without exception, serial killers are male, because even in the rare instances when women kill multiple victims sequentially, they lack a "sexualized" motivation. Not everyone agrees. Criminology professor Eric W. Hickey, for example, calls "myopic" the view that because women kill in different ways and for different reasons they aren't really serial killers. In his 1997 book *Serial Killers and Their Victims*, Hickey identifies 62 female serial murderers since 1826, including 27 who murdered in 1995. At the very least, however, the overwhelming majority of serial killers are men.

Geographically, serial killers are found on every continent except Antarctica, with North America having 79 percent of the world total and Europe running a distant second with 17 percent. The United States alone accounts for about three-quarters of the world's reported total of serial murders—an alarming statistic, to be sure—but part of that is attributable to the greater sophistication of American law enforcement agencies in identifying serial killings. Developing nations account for a mere 3 percent of the reported world total, a fact that can be explained by cultural factors, poor communication, and news censorship.

In recent years law enforcement professionals and behavioral scientists have recognized that serial killers—wherever they are found—act from fundamentally different motivations than do other murderers. For the serial murderer, killing is not a crime of passion or a means to get money or the unintended consequence of another crime. Rather, it is the culmination of an overpowering urge that has been growing—sometimes for years—until the ritual of murder has been integrated into the killer's life. It is as though the serial murderer lives to kill.

WHERE DO THEY COME FROM?

ntoning the words of the Twenty-third Psalm—
"The Lord is my shepherd; I shall not want. / In
verdant pastures he gives me repose. . . ."—John
Wayne Gacy would slowly strangle the handcuffed boy
or young man he had lured into his suburban Chicago
house. When the victim was close to death, Gacy
would loosen the rope to inflict another round of beat-
ing and sodomy on him before tightening the noose
again. Gacy buried the bodies of his victims—29 in
all—in the crawl space under his house until he ran out
of room there.

Athletic, popular, and a good student, Herbert Mullin was voted "most likely to succeed" by his high school classmates. His descent into madness would culminate in the slaying of 14 victims.

On May 7, 1972, Edmund Emil Kemper, 24,
stopped his car along the side of a California highway
to pick up two female hitchhikers. The women, students at California's Fresno State College, were travel-
ing to Palo Alto to visit friends at Stanford. But they

never made it. Kemper drove the women to a secluded spot and stabbed them to death. Then he took his victims' bodies to his mother's house, where he photographed and dissected them. Before turning himself in nearly a year later, Kemper killed six more women, decapitating, mutilating, and performing sex acts on the corpses, then scattering the body parts. His second-to-last victim was his mother.

For years Jerome Brudos had been breaking into homes and stealing women's clothing. He'd started exclusively with high-heeled shoes but eventually expanded his thefts to include underwear. Although he had assaulted women before, Brudos had never killed anyone until a 19-year-old woman selling encyclopedias door-to-door appeared at his house one night in 1968. After she was dead, he cut off her left foot and placed it in one of his favorite high-heeled shoes. Over the next few months, he murdered several other women and hung their bodies in his garage, where he dressed them in outfits he had stolen and photographed them before dismembering and disposing of the bodies. Brudos stored body parts he particularly liked in a locked freezer.

Richard Trenton Chase believed he was being poisoned with an agent known only to him, a substance that was turning his blood to powder. Unless he obtained fresh blood, he would die. He found some near his apartment in Sacramento, California, when he entered the home of a pregnant young woman, killed her, horribly mutilated the body, and evidently collected some of the victim's blood in a yogurt container and drank it. Three days later, Chase entered another home in the area and shot and killed a man, two children, and a woman. Once again, the woman's body was grotesquely mutilated and her blood apparently drunk.

Gacy, Kemper, Brudos, Chase. Four serial killers whose horrifying acts stagger the imagination and lead inevitably to a question: Where do murderers like these come from? As with other complex human behavior, definitive answers are elusive. While there is near-universal agreement that the behaviors and

Sheriff's deputies remove 1 of 29 bodies buried in the crawl space beneath the suburban Chicago house of John Wayne Gacy.

thought patterns that lead to serial murder develop over a long period and usually begin in childhood, experts point to different causes. Most likely various factors are involved. But, as the following cases illustrate, in their backgrounds and in their crimes serial killers aren't all alike.

Traumatic abuse in childhood has long been viewed as a primary cause of violent behavior in adulthood. And John Wayne Gacy, born in 1942, certainly experienced such abuse. Gacy's father, an alcoholic, would come home from work and ensconce himself in the basement, where he would drink. Anyone who disturbed him was chased away with a torrent of threats and verbal abuse. After working himself into a drunken rage, Gacy's father would emerge from the basement to berate and beat his wife and children.

Because serial murder is strongly linked to sexual deviancy, many killers commit rape or sexual assault before they begin murdering. Gacy's history of molesting boys and young men dates back at least to 1968, when, as the manager of a fast-food restaurant in Iowa, he handcuffed an employee in a back room and attempted to force sex on him. Sentenced to 10 years in prison for the incident, Gacy served just 18 months before being released.

After moving to Illinois, Gacy ran afoul of the law once again. In 1972 a young man claimed that Gacy, now a building contractor, had picked him up, taken him to his house, and assaulted him. Gacy claimed that the young man was merely trying to extort money from him, and the charges were eventually dropped.

After this incident, Gacy became, by all outward appearances, a pillar of the community. His construction business boomed. He married for the second time, and his wife, her children from a previous marriage, and her mother all moved into his cozy suburban Chicago house. Gacy was active in the Democratic Party. He dressed as a clown to entertain children at charitable

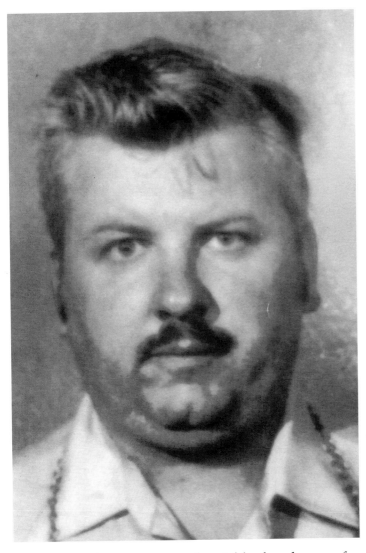

events. He threw an annual neighborhood party for hundreds of guests.

Years later, Gacy would recall that his first killing occurred in 1972, but he claimed that it had been in self-defense: a young man with whom he had had sex attacked him with a knife, Gacy said. He buried the body in the crawl space underneath his house, pouring concrete over it when his wife complained of unpleasant odors in the home.

Sometime after this first, supposedly unpremeditated killing, Gacy began actively seeking victims. Initially he found them in the transient homosexual districts of Chicago. Later he found them on busy streets or even among the part-time employees of his construction company.

When his wife and family were away, Gacy would pick up a young man on the pretext of paying him for sex or offering him a construction job, take the man to his house, and ply him with liquor. Then he would immobilize his victim, often by offering to show the man a rope or handcuff "trick." Once his victim had been rendered helpless, Gacy sodomized, beat, and suffocated or strangled him until the victim was on the verge of death. Then he revived the victim to inflict more torture, eventually killing by strangulation. Gacy buried the bodies of his victims in the crawl space.

After his wife left him in 1976, the killings escalated. By the time he was caught in December of 1978, Gacy had claimed 33 victims.

Where did Gacy the killer come from? Beaten and abused as a child by a father whose rages were fueled by alcohol consumed in the basement, John Wayne Gacy grew up to abuse and kill young men—and bury them beneath his own house. The parallels are too striking to ignore. And Gacy would violently strike the genitalia of his victims while slowly strangling them, a fact that has led some analysts to conclude that he killed to symbolically recover the masculine power that his father had taken from him.

In the late 1970s Robert Ressler, an FBI agent who taught courses for law enforcement professionals in the bureau's National Academy, launched a groundbreaking study of violent criminals. Called the Criminal Personality Research Project (CPRP), the study was the first systematic examination of serial murderers, and extensive interviews with the killers were a key component. Among the murderers Ressler and his colleagues interviewed, nearly 70 percent had a familial history of drug or alcohol abuse, and about 4 in 10 reported being physically abused or beaten during childhood. So in this respect, John Wayne Gacy is not unusual among serial killers.

Unlike Gacy, Ed Kemper wasn't physically abused during childhood. But he did suffer emotional abuse, a background shared by virtually all the serial murderers in the CPRP. His parents fought constantly, and his mother, Clarnell, seems to have resented him because he looked so much like his father. When he was 10, Clarnell made her son sleep in the basement, saying she feared he would sexually molest his sisters. Each night before she went to bed, Kemper's mother closed the basement door, leaving him in the darkness—isolated, afraid, and angry.

After his parents separated, Kemper killed and mutilated two family cats, and his mother sent him to live with his father. But he was unhappy there and soon ran away to return to his mother. Within the space of four years, Clarnell Kemper twice remarried and divorced. During this period, implying that he was the cause of her troubles, she frequently shipped her son off to his grandparents' farm, which he detested. Kemper was a shy child, and this, combined with his enormous size—as an adult he reached 6'9" and weighed 300 pounds—always made him somewhat of a freak among his peers. When he lived at his grandparents' farm, his classmates were particularly cruel in their ostracism.

It was at the farm, when he was just 15, that Kemper killed his grandparents after a squabble with his grandmother. Then he called his mother, who had just remarried, to tell her that she'd have to cut short her honeymoon because he had shot his grandparents.

Kemper received four years of treatment in a mental hospital before being released into a probationary program. A year later he was paroled into his mother's custody. Although she continued to blame him for her

Edmund Emil Kemper III, "the Coed Killer" of Santa Cruz, California. Kemper's serial murder spree ended only after he had killed his mother—the real object, experts have concluded, of his rage.

problems, Clarnell tried to have her son's juvenile record expunged so that he could pursue a career with the California Highway Patrol.

He was rejected for the highway patrol, but Kemper did get a job with the state highway department, which gave him the opportunity to associate with state troopers. After he had embarked on his serial murder spree, Kemper followed the progress of the "Coed Killer" investigation through his law enforcement contacts.

The murders began when, storming out of his mother's house one night in 1972 after a particularly vitriolic argument, Kemper decided he was going to kill the first pretty woman he encountered. Not much is known about the victim, and her body was never found.

Kemper's next victims were the hitchhiking students from Fresno State. A few months after that, he picked up another hitchhiker, a 15-year-old girl, whom he suffocated. He had sex with the corpse and, once again, took the body home for dissection. The next day, Kemper had an appointment with state psychiatrists, who were still evaluating the appropriateness of sealing his juvenile record. In his book *Mind Hunter*, John Douglas, formerly the FBI's chief criminal profiler, describes what happened at that appointment.

[The victim's] head was lying in his car trunk. The interview went well, though, and the psychiatrists declared him no longer a threat to himself or others and recommended that his juvenile record be sealed. Kemper reveled in this brilliantly symbolic act. It demonstrated his contempt for the system and his superiority to it at the same time.

Kemper found his next victim at the University of California at Santa Cruz, where his mother worked as an administrative assistant. (She had gotten him a university parking sticker so that he could pick her up after work, enabling him to move around the campus without arousing suspicion.) He buried the young woman's head outside his mother's bedroom window.

One night about a month later, Kemper picked up two female students on the Santa Cruz campus, shot them in his car, and covered their bodies with blankets. As he approached a security booth on the edge of the campus, both women were still alive and groaning. But it was dark, and Kemper calmly told the guards that the young ladies had had too much to drink. At his mother's house, he performed his usual ritual of sex with the corpses, decapitation, and dismemberment. Later, as he had done with the others, he disposed of the victims' body parts in various remote locations to hinder identification.

Before dawn on the morning of April 21, 1973, Kemper crept into his mother's bedroom as she slept and smashed her head with a hammer, an act he had fantasized about for years. Then he slit her throat and decapitated her, cutting out her larynx—her voice box—and attempting to grind it up in the garbage disposal. But the garbage disposal only spit the larynx out, and, as Kemper observed ruefully after his arrest, even though he had killed his mother "she was still bitching at me. I couldn't get her to shut up!"

After abusing his mother's corpse, Kemper wrapped it in a sheet and stuffed it into a closet. Then he invited a friend of his mother's to the house to help plan a "surprise party." He strangled her, cut off her head, and stuffed her body into another closet.

For some reason, Kemper didn't attempt to conceal his last two killings—perhaps he felt that would be futile, as any police investigation into his mother's dis-appearance would focus on him. At any rate, he left Santa Cruz and headed eastward, fully expecting to hear news of his mother's murder on the car radio. Hearing nothing, he decided to turn himself in. From Pueblo, Colorado, he called the Santa Cruz Police Department and confessed that he was the notorious Coed Killer, then waited until the authorities arrived to take him into custody.

According to former FBI profiler John Douglas, "Kemper's overriding fantasy [had been] to rid himself of his domineering, abusive mother, and everything he did as a killer can be analyzed in that context." In Kemper, Douglas sees "an example of someone not born a serial killer but manufactured as one."

If Ed Kemper the serial killer was "manufactured" by his mother's emotional abuse, the case of Jerome Brudos seems less clear-cut. At the age of five, Brudos found a pair of women's high-heeled shoes in a dump near his home. Fascinated, he took them home and tried them on. His mother, a strict and domineering woman, angri-ly demanded that he get rid of the shoes, but instead Brudos hid them. What about the high heels so enthralled the five-year-old? It's impossible to know, but presumably his interest preceded his mother's angry reaction. At any rate, his mother eventually found the forbidden shoes, burned them, and punished Brudos. But this didn't extinguish the young boy's fascination with high heels. Soon he stole his teacher's shoes.

By the age of 13, Brudos had begun abducting girls and taking them to the barn on his family's farm, where he made them take off their clothes. After he had pho-tographed a girl naked, Brudos would lock the door and leave. A short while later, dressed in different clothes, he would return, claiming to be Jerome's twin brother, Ed. After asking the girl what had happened, he would confide that Jerome was in therapy and that he, Ed, hoped she wouldn't report him because that might set

Homicide investigators outside the house of Ed Kemper's mother. In a macabre joke, Kemper had buried the head of one of his victims, with the face toward his mother's bedroom window, in this spot because, he declared, she had always "wanted people to look up to her."

his progress back. The ploy invariably worked, probably because the girls were young and had not been physically harmed.

Brudos began breaking into houses to steal women's shoes and, later, underwear, which he would take home and try on. At 17 he was arrested for assaulting a girl in his car; he had picked her up and wanted to see her naked. After a few months in a mental hospital, he was released, and he resumed his raids for women's clothing. But whereas before he had taken care to avoid breaking into houses when the occupants were home, now he often confronted the women whose clothes he was stealing. Sometimes he even choked them until they were unconscious.

Typically, a serial killer's aberrant fantasies and antisocial behavior begin in childhood and escalate over the course of years. Jerome Brudos provides a good example. As a child of five, he became fascinated by women's shoes. When his mother destroyed the pair he had found, he stole a pair from his teacher. By early adolescence he was abducting girls so that he could photograph them naked. He began breaking into houses to steal women's clothing, at first when no one was home, but later when they were, and he then had to assault the women to get their clothes.

But Brudos had not yet taken the ultimate step. He would do that in 1968, before his 30th birthday, when his wife and two children were away and the young encyclopedia salesperson showed up at his door.

In his book *Whoever Fights Monsters*, Robert Ressler describes the path serial killers take from violent fantasy to deadly reality, from less serious offenses to murder. Ressler calls the final step "crossing-the-line behavior," and though the killer has been heading toward it for some time, he generally crosses the line somewhat tentatively.

> [Crossing-the-line behavior] entails the offender doing
> things that he actually knows are wrong, and that will

bring him untold grief if he is caught. Yet he is impelled to cross the line by everything that has previously occurred in his life. Only later, after many such acts, will he come to believe that he is invincible and will never be caught. Just before he edges to the line, the young man isn't so certain.

Jerome Brudos crossed the line when a vulnerable victim unexpectedly presented herself. If his story can be believed, John Wayne Gacy crossed the line when he killed a lover in self-defense. But for other serial killers, crossing the line involves more of a conscious choice. Ed Kemper, for example, set out to kill the first attractive woman he found after a bad argument with his mother.

In the aftermath of his first killing, the serial murderer is likely to discover that he actually enjoyed the experience, and he relishes the thought of additional, more elaborate, and more emotionally satisfying murders. This is what Jerome Brudos did.

Brudos placed classified ads for amateur models in local papers. When a woman answered, he would arrange to meet her in a motel. The lucky women he simply paid to model panty hose and high heels for his photographs. But over the course of several months he abducted three of the models, took them to his house, and murdered them. In his garage, he dressed the bodies in his favorite outfits, particularly shoes, and photographed them. Then he dismembered them and disposed of the body parts he didn't want. He stored the other body parts, including breasts from which he made molds, in a locked freezer in the garage. On a few occasions his wife remarked to friends that whenever she wanted to cook a roast, Jerome insisted on getting the meat from the freezer for her.

Unlike Jerome Brudos, whose bizarre later behavior appears to have its origins in his early fixation on a pair of high heels, Richard Trenton Chase seems to have had an unremarkable childhood. Born in 1950, Chase

As a child of five, Jerome Brudos (above) brought home a pair of high-heeled shoes he'd found in a dump. This was the beginning of a lifelong obsession that eventually led Brudos to serial murder.

grew up in a middle-class family and was a cooperative child. However, as with half of the murderers studied in the CPRP, there was mental illness in Chase's immediate family: his mother was a schizophrenic.

When he was about 12, his parents began to have marital difficulties, and during their frequent arguments, Chase's mother often accused his father of trying to poison her, of using illicit drugs, and of being unfaithful to her. Eventually they divorced and Mrs. Chase remarried.

In high school, Chase was an undistinguished student. During those years he began drinking and taking drugs, and at one point he was sentenced to community service work for possession of marijuana. After graduating from high school in 1969, Chase briefly attended a community college but soon dropped out.

Unable to hold a job and support himself, Chase alternated between living at his father's house and staying with his mother. His parents were having more and more difficulty keeping him out of trouble, and his mental state was deteriorating. In 1972 he was arrested for drunk driving. The next year he was picked up for carrying a handgun without a license and resisting arrest. In 1976 he tried to inject himself with rabbit's blood.

That incident got Chase committed to a mental institution, but his behavior there was no less bizarre. He would, for example, bite off the heads of birds he had caught, and he may also have been trapping small animals and drinking their blood. Though Chase was a paranoid schizophrenic, staff psychiatrists decided to release him in 1977 after concluding that medication was controlling his condition.

He spent some time after his release with both of his parents, but mostly Chase was alone in the apartment that his mother had secured for him. His mental illness continued to make it impossible for him to work.

Near Lake Tahoe in August 1977, Chase was picked

up by authorities because his clothes were soaked with blood and he had a bucket of blood in his truck. Chase claimed he had been hunting, and, because the blood in the bucket came from a cow, he was released.

Between August and December, Chase bought or abducted a number of dogs and cats. It seems probable that he killed them all to drink their blood.

In December he bought a handgun, lying about his history of mental illness on the application. He fired shots at several houses before hitting and killing a man who was unloading groceries from his car.

On January 28, 1978, Chase began the most gruesome phase of his quest for blood when he killed a pregnant young woman in her home and severely mutilated the body. The woman's intestines were exposed, several internal organs were cut out, some body parts were missing, and blood had apparently been collected and drunk.

Three days later Chase struck again, entering another house and shooting four more people. Once again, he mutilated the body of the only woman present, and he seems to have sexually assaulted the body as well. Chase took car keys from one of the victims, and police later found the vehicle in the middle of a street not far away. The driver's-side door was open, the keys were in the ignition, and the engine was still running.

When the police caught Chase two days later and searched his apartment, they found bloody rags, knives, blenders containing blood, and various human organs. Ominously, the word *today* was written on a calendar on the dates of Chase's murders and on 44 other dates throughout the year, indicating, perhaps, that Chase intended to kill 44 more times in 1978.

When Robert Ressler interviewed him in prison for the CPRP, Chase explained that his killings had been in self-defense. Because he was a victim of "soap-dish poisoning"—as evidenced by the gooey residue that was always in his soap dish—he needed fresh blood or

With the Vietnam War winding down in late 1972, Herbert Mullin (shown here being led into court) worried that nature wasn't getting the blood sacrifices it required. To help avert a natural disaster, he embarked on a killing spree. Psychotics like Mullin account for a percentage of serial killers, but experts believe that most serial murders are committed by men who have a clear perception of reality and aren't legally insane.

his own blood would turn to powder and he would die. In fact, UFOs had commanded him, via telepathy, to kill, Chase revealed. He also said that he entered only houses with unlocked doors because "if the door is locked, that means you're not welcome."

The four cases discussed above are representative of the variation in the backgrounds and criminal behavior of serial killers. They hint at the difficulty of finding one key cause, or set of causes, to explain where every serial murderer comes from.

Establishing a definitive cause is perhaps easiest with murderers like Richard Trenton Chase and Herbert Mullin, who killed 14 people in California on the supposed telepathic instructions of his father, an army officer, because he believed that nature demanded human blood or an environmental catastrophe would ensue. These men were paranoid schizophrenics; they suffered from a full-blown mental illness characterized by delusions and hallucinations. In short, they had completely lost touch with reality. While people suffering from psychoses such as paranoid schizophrenia aren't usually a threat to others, they do constitute a portion of serial murderers, and because their thinking is so delusional, their crimes can be extremely bizarre.

But most serial murderers aren't classified as psychotics but rather as psychopaths—their perception of reality is clear except that they feel no social or moral obligations. What, then, is the origin of their behavior? Childhood abuse has long been linked to the creation of serial murderers. Often, as in the case of John Wayne Gacy, this abuse is physical or sexual. As previously indicated, some 40 percent of the killers in the CPRP reported being physically abused or beaten as children; in addition, more than 70 percent reported witnessing or experiencing sexually stressful events, including being molested or raped by family members or strangers. But, as we have seen, the abuse suffered in childhood by a serial murderer need not be physical or sexual. The case of Ed Kemper shows that purely emotional abuse can also be devastating. And neglect, too, must be considered a form of emotional abuse. When a child's needs and actions are consistently ignored, the child is likely to grow up unable to understand or respect the boundaries between his own needs and the rights of others, and indeed, several known serial murderers have grown up in profoundly neglectful environments.

For David Heise, professor of sociology at Indiana University at Bloomington, the common denominator is that every serial killer has been "socially assassinated" in the early years of life by factors he could not control. Consider Henry Lee Lucas, a killer whose precise body count remains unknown. The victim of childhood beatings, Lucas was subjected to cross-dressing, blinded in one eye, forced to witness his mother's sexuality, and taught sadistic bestiality (sex with animals) by her lovers; he was drinking heavily by age 9 or 10. Or Ottis Toole, a drifter who left a trail of murder across the South. Dressed as a girl and raped as a child, Toole was torn between his grandmother's Satanism and his mother's fanatical Christianity. Or Charles Manson, who inspired his followers to murder and mutilate seven victims in two nights of gruesome savagery. The illegitimate son of a prostitute who abandoned him, Manson was humiliated almost from the moment of his birth—brutalized by his uncle, forced to wear a dress to school, and raped, he was living on the streets at the age of 10.

These are extreme examples, of course, and not every serial killer comes from a background as troubled as these. But abuse of some kind figures in the childhoods of the vast majority of people who go on to become serial killers. This leads to a perplexing question. If childhood abuse is really the key to what makes a serial murderer, then given the extent of abuse in our society, why aren't there *more* serial murderers?

Brain damage or neurological impairment has been offered as another possible explanation for serial murder. The evidence at this point is anecdotal but tantalizing. Ottis Toole suffered seizures as a child. A battery of neurological tests and X rays conducted on Henry Lee Lucas at the direction of psychologist Joel Norris revealed damage to areas of the brain that control violent behavior and the ability to manage emotions; Lucas had sustained serious head traumas from the

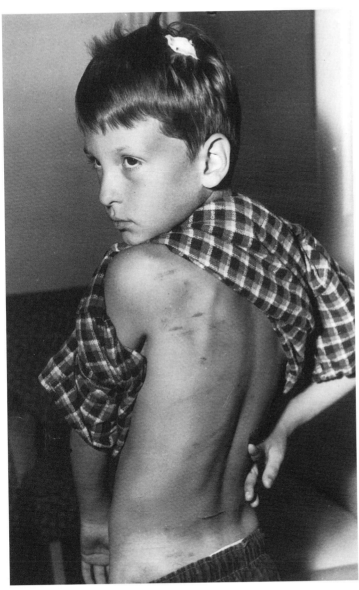

Each day, as many as 7,000 cases of child abuse and neglect are reported in the United States, according to the Children's Defense Fund. Such abuse plays an important role in the development of serial murderers.

childhood beatings he had endured. An autopsy conducted on Charles Whitman, whose 90-minute shooting spree from the Texas Tower in 1966 left 16 people dead, revealed a tumor in one of the temporal lobes of his brain. Because his killings occurred during one incident, Whitman is considered a mass murderer, not a serial killer. But some experts have wondered

Convicted killer Henry Lee Lucas. Neurological tests and X rays revealed that Lucas had damage to areas of the brain involved in controlling violent behavior and managing emotions. Could brain damage, tumors, or organic conditions such as epilepsy provide at least a partial explanation for the behavior of many serial killers? The evidence at this point is inconclusive.

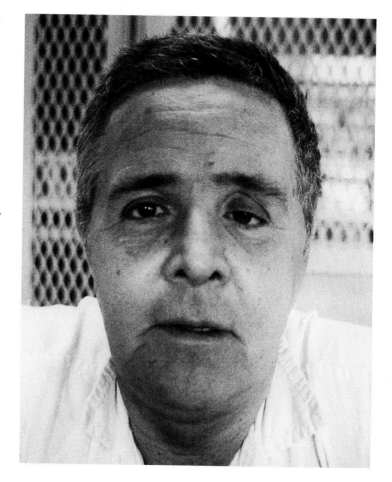

whether similar organic conditions in the brain might help to explain the behavior of serial murderers—murderers such as Arthur Shawcross, who killed as many as 11 prostitutes and homeless women in the Rochester, New York, area and was found to have a cyst on his temporal lobe.

Dr. Dorothy Lewis, a psychiatrist and researcher at the New York University School of Medicine, has made the case that much—perhaps even most—violent criminal behavior is caused by a physical or organic condition, such as epilepsy, a head injury, or a brain tumor or cyst, in combination with abuse or a traumatic event in childhood. At the serial murder trial of Shawcross, Lewis testified that his cyst produced a kind of epilepsy that, combined with post-traumatic stress disorder and the intense physical and sexual abuse his mother had inflicted on him, rendered Shawcross unable to control his violent urges and essentially unaware of what he was doing.

Other research has linked certain violent behavior to hereditary factors—for example, genetic defects that produce abnormal levels of the neurochemicals serotonin and norepinephrine, which may predispose a person, some studies have indicated, to impulsive aggression, uncontrollable rages, or premeditated cruelty. The extent to which these, or similar inherited characteristics, play a role in the making of serial murderers in particular has not been established.

But the hypothesis that environmental factors such as severe childhood abuse or trauma produce a serial killer only when combined with brain conditions or genetic abnormalities offers one explanation for why there aren't more serial killers. For serial murder experts like Robert Ressler and John Douglas, however, the real explanation lies elsewhere. The key, they maintain, is fantasy. Unlike others who come from similar backgrounds, children who go on to become serial murderers retreat into a world of bizarre, violent, sexual fantasies.

As adolescents, Ressler says, they overcompensate "for the aggression in their early lives by repeating the abuse in fantasy—but, this time, with themselves as the aggressors." And eventually—generally after they are adults and a stressful event has occurred—they "make happen in the real world what they [have] seen over and over again in their minds": they murder.

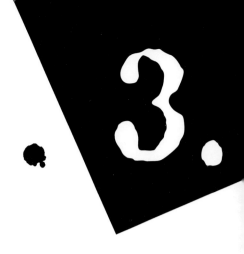

INTO THE ABYSS

A deputy sheriff gazes into the grave of a serial killer's victim near Yuba City, California.

He may seem withdrawn or gregarious, but emotionally he is profoundly isolated. He may be employed, may even be successful in business, but it's just as likely that, if he's working at all, it's in a job he considers below his capabilities. He might have an extraordinary intellect, or he might be of average or slightly below average intelligence. Maybe he has a wife or girlfriend, or maybe he shrinks from contact with women, but in any case he is incapable of sustaining a long-term, consensual, adult relationship. This is true regardless of whether he is heterosexual or homosexual.

For years he has had sexual fantasies. But they haven't been like the fantasies of his peers, who envision themselves, for example, sexually satisfying a supermodel. No, his fantasies have involved raping, debasing, dominating, and brutalizing. And his fantasies haven't been occasional; they've become an integral part of his life, actually substituting for inter-

Ted Bundy (center) confers with his defense team at the start of his 1979 trial for the murder of two Florida State University students.

personal relationships. Over the years these fantasies have evolved in detail and in violence. Now he imagines himself killing his partner in a specific manner.

Chances are, he's already gotten into trouble with the law. And just as his fantasies have evolved, so too has the seriousness of his offenses escalated.

His first murder will probably, but not necessarily, follow some stressful situation in his life. Maybe he'll be fired from his job or will suffer a financial setback of some kind. Maybe his wife or girlfriend will leave him. Maybe he'll have a bad argument with his mother. And all the anger he has toward his parents, toward women, toward society in general will be unleashed on a stranger.

This is a typical scenario for how a man—and, as previously stated, the vast majority of serial killers are men—will plunge into the abyss of serial murder.

By definition, the serial killer doesn't stop after his first murder. Finding emotional satisfaction in the act, he relives the killing in his mind and eventually fantasizes about another murder. Typically, a serial killer refines his fantasies as he commits each murder, and his skill at carrying out his crimes increases as well. As John Douglas writes in *Mind Hunter,* for most serial killers "the hunting and killing is the most important thing in their lives, their main 'job,' so they're thinking about it all the time."

Douglas reports that Ed Kemper, a highly intelligent man, thought long and hard about how best to put potential victims at ease until he had them in a vulnerable position. When he picked up a hitchhiker, for example, Kemper would ask where she was going, then glance at his watch as though he had an important appointment to keep. This would give the woman the impression that he had a lot more on his mind than her, when in fact killing her and getting away with it was all he was thinking about. Because they are so focused on

Three of Bundy's victims, showing his preference for pretty young women with long hair parted in the middle. The selection of a specific type of victim, and the use of guile in trapping the victim, are hallmarks of organized serial killers.

their "job," and because quite often they are astute judges of human behavior, serial killers—especially "organized" killers like Kemper—frequently enjoy a tremendous advantage over their potential victims.

"Organized" and "disorganized" are the two broad categories that law enforcement uses to classify serial killers. The categories embrace personality characteristics as well as specific behavioral manifestations. Although the categories are useful in understanding—and therefore combating—different serial killers, it should be noted that they aren't perfect. They fit most, not all, of the cases, and a third classification, "mixed," refers to offenders who display important characteristics of both the organized and disorganized type.

The hallmark of the organized serial murderer is logic. Organized killers plan their crimes methodically. They take whatever "tools" they need—ropes, handcuffs, tape—with them when they search for a victim. They have a weapon ready, and they take it with them after the crime. Organized killers avoid leaving clues at a crime scene. To this end, most hide their victims' bodies, and many will even dismember the bodies and dispose of the various parts at different locations to hinder identification. Organized killers also tend to wipe away fingerprints and blood, to take the victim's clothes, and to commit the actual murder in a different location from where they leave the body. All of this makes gathering evidence more difficult.

By contrast, disorganized killers don't plan their crimes and don't go to great lengths to conceal their tracks. The victim's body is often left at the scene of the murder, where police are more able to recover important evidence such as fingerprints, hair samples, and semen. Disorganized killers often use a weapon they've taken from the victim and leave it with the body; it may have fingerprints on it.

In the selection of victims, organized and disorganized killers differ fundamentally. Whereas the disorganized killer tends to prey on random victims, the organized killer searches for a specific kind of victim, based on his fantasies. Richard Trenton Chase, a disorganized killer, simply wandered into houses that were unlocked. Ted Bundy, on the other hand, searched college campuses and selected pretty young women with long hair parted in the middle—women who reminded him, it is speculated, of the fiancée who had broken up with him. Organized and disorganized killers also gain control of their victims in different manners. The organized killer typically employs verbal skills and guile to maneuver a victim into a vulnerable position before springing his trap; the disorganized killer generally overwhelms his victims with a sudden, incapacitating onslaught that authorities refer to as a blitz-style attack.

Serial murder is considered sexually based homicide, even when the killer has no overt sexual contact with the victim. This is because sexually deviant fantasy plays a vital role in the crime. David Berkowitz, for example, never got near his victims, shooting them with a powerful handgun as they sat in cars. But after a killing, Berkowitz would return to his home and masturbate, and he also experienced sexual excitement when he thought about his crimes or returned to the crime scenes. Serial killers are, without exception, considered sexually maladjusted.

If sex is at the heart of serial murder, the sexual practices of organized and disorganized killers are notably different. Organized murderers personalize their victims, selecting a particular type and usually raping or torturing them while the victims are alive. Even those who are impotent under normal conditions are able to perform sex acts when abusing a particular victim. Disorganized killers, on the other hand, depersonalize their victims. If they have sex with a victim, it is usually only after the victim is dead or unconscious, and frequently the victim is mutilated after death. Once again, it should be noted that the characteristics

An employee of the Los Angeles County Coroner's Office and two investigators from the Hillside Strangler task force examine a crime scene. The victim is in the trunk of the car. Organized killers tend to go to great lengths to conceal their victims' bodies, whereas disorganized killers do not.

of organized and disorganized killers are only generally applicable. Ed Kemper, for instance, is considered an organized killer because of the great degree of planning in his crimes, but he also displayed the disorganized characteristic of having sex with victims only after they were dead.

Organized offenders tend to be more intelligent, more verbal, and more attractive than disorganized ones. For this reason, they often have had romantic partners, but long-term, consensual relationships are never satisfying, because they don't provide what the organized killer really wants. That, according to profiler John Douglas, is most often domination, manipulation, and control.

The organized serial murderer closely follows media accounts of his crimes and of the police investigations. And he strives to improve with each murder, taking pride in his cleverness and skill. In many cases organized killers consider themselves superior to nearly everyone, including those who are trying to catch them.

The typical disorganized offender, on the other hand, feels inferior to nearly everyone. Often he has some physical deformity or another embarrassing condition, such as severe stuttering, that makes social contacts painful, so he withdraws from society. As a rule, disorganized offenders don't have romantic relationships, and they usually shun contact with women. Unlike their organized counterparts, they take little interest in their murders after committing them. Some analysts interpret their crimes as a rejection of the society they feel has rejected them.

A percentage of disorganized offenders are psychotics—that is, like Richard Trenton Chase and Herbert Mullin, they suffer from a severe, full-blown mental illness and have completely lost touch with reality. In such cases the motivations for committing the murders vary with the given offender's particular delusions.

Robert Ressler placed about two-thirds of the serial killers he studied in the organized category, though, for reasons that will be discussed later, he believes that the number and percentage of organized offenders is growing. Regardless of whether an individual serial murderer is organized or disorganized, however, the overwhelming compulsion he feels makes it a near certainty that he'll continue to kill until he is stopped.

THE RITUAL
PHASES

A serial murderer's compulsion to kill may be likened to an addiction, not only to the crime itself but also to a specific pattern of fantasy and violence that becomes the killer's way of life. Serial murderers make the act of killing into a ritual, a way to preserve the murder—and the emotional and sexual gratification it provides—in the killer's mind. The particular victims, the preparations for their capture and torture, their deaths, and the disposal of their remains all have relevance to the killer's behavior.

This need for ritual is a way to identify that a serial killer is at work; it sets him apart from other murderers. The sequence of the ritual is the killer's way of working up the "murder high." Psychologist Joel Norris and other experts have broken the ritual of serial murder into the following seven phases:

1. The Aura Phase

In the aura phase, Norris says, the killer experiences a certain withdrawal from reality that indicates the beginning of a behavior change. First, time seems to

In the aura phase—the first stage in psychologist Joel Norris's conception of the ritual phases of serial murder—the killer experiences a withdrawal from reality as time seems to slow down and the senses become heightened.

slow down. The senses become heightened; sounds and colors are more vivid, the sense of smell becomes more intense, and the killer's skin becomes more sensitive to touch. The killer needs to find a "companion," at first a make-believe companion, to play a role in his ritual. This is the aura state, the fantasy state, and the hallucination, Norris believes, can last for a minute or two or for several months—until the killer begins to hunt for a victim, a real companion.

The aura phase can also be a prolonged fantasy, with the killer acting out the entire crime, step by step, in his mind. In this way, the killer can play the fantasy over and over for weeks, months, or even years at a time—until he is ready to find an actual person to become an actual victim. Then the fantasy is over and the trolling phase begins.

2. The Trolling Phase

In the trolling phase, the killer actively begins searching for a real victim. Especially in the case of an organized killer, his fantasies will dictate where he should search for the type of victim he is looking for. Different serial killers favor different spots: the parking lots of shopping malls, dark city streets where single people are likely to walk at night, the dormitories and student centers of a large university, elementary school playgrounds, schools for the deaf or mentally retarded. But the fact that a killer has previously selected all of his victims from the same setting is no guarantee that he will continue to do so. Organized offenders can adapt their behavior to different circumstances.

In the trolling phase the killer becomes very alert and focused on finding his victim. But in most cases there is no outward indication of his intentions; organized killers in the trolling phase generally function with considerable cunning. Ted Bundy, for example, appeared charming and friendly. His arm in a sling, he lured his victims into his car by asking for help with

books, packages, even the hull of a sailboat. The few victims who escaped this ploy reported that Bundy never seemed out of control. Strangler Carlton Gary kept watch on his intended victims' houses for weeks, memorizing their schedules and habits so that when he did strike, he was able to act fearlessly, knowing when his victims would be alone and vulnerable.

3. The Wooing Phase

Most organized serial killers capture their victims by winning their confidence and luring them into a trap. John Wayne Gacy was able to do this by promising his victims jobs in his company or cash for sexual favors—sometimes even by becoming a father figure. The victims of an organized serial killer rarely seem to have put up a fight, indicating that the killer chose a victim whom he could control with little difficulty. Inexperienced killers and those with profound feelings of inadequacy tend to favor the most vulnerable victims—the young, the elderly, the handicapped. Disor-

Where a serial murderer trolls for his victims is often dictated by the killer's fantasies. But there is no guarantee that, for example, a killer who abducted five previous victims from a playground will go back to a playground to find his sixth victim. Many serial killers adapt their modus operandi.

ganized killers, on the other hand, don't select their victims logically, and in many cases the victim appears to have put up a fight before succumbing.

4. Capture

This is a moment many serial killers savor because they believe they have closed off all possibility of the victim's escape and can take all the time they want to prepare the victim for the ritual of murder. It can happen as fast as the locking of a car door or a quick blow to the head, or the killer can talk at length to his victim about what is about to take place. Ted Bundy kept charming his victims until he reached one of his "safe places," a place where he and the victim were completely isolated. Then he raped and beat them to death.

5. The Murder

The murder phase, Norris believes, is a ritual reenactment of the awful experiences of the killer's childhood. Only this time the killer tries to reverse the roles. In this way he seeks to magically cancel out his earlier suffering and establish his own power and identity. Henry Lee Lucas and Ottis Toole, for example, burned their victims with cigarettes and white-hot metal, abuse that had been inflicted on them as children. For Lucas, the act of mutilation was the high point of the ritual, although most confessed serial killers cite the moment of the murder as their emotional high point.

6. The Totem Phase

The emotional high that the killer experiences at the moment of his victim's death fades quickly. Some serial killers try to prolong the feeling of power and control by dismembering the body and using parts as mementos or souvenirs. These body parts may be buried in isolated spots to which the killer might return, or they might be preserved in jars or scrapbooks. Some serial killers even eat parts of their victims' remains.

Others take jewelry or clothing from their victims or photograph the murder. Leonard Lake, a Vietnam veteran who murdered as many as 25 people, videotaped the minutes leading up to his victims' deaths; Jerome Brudos photographed his victims' bodies after he had dressed them in his favorite outfits.

This is the totem phase, in which the victim has become a symbol of what the murderer hoped he would attain from the killing—power, control, an emotional release of his past, the fulfillment of a fantasy. The killer hopes to relive the "glory" of the actual murder by replaying it in his mind, and the mementos are props. But the actual murder is never as perfect as the fantasy, and the killer ultimately doesn't achieve the power he sought. Eventually, Norris believes, depression sets in.

7. The Depression Phase

Ted Bundy confessed that he never really got what he had hoped for out of his murders. Henry Lee Lucas reported the same thing. The reason for this is simple: the killer is merely acting out a ritualistic fantasy. He cannot erase his past or his anger or his inadequacy by the act of murder. After the killing, the identity of the victim is lost, and the victim no longer represents what the killer thought he or she would. No real power is achieved, and the killer is left feeling empty, depressed, and damned.

For days or weeks after the most recent murder, the killer may be in a depressive state. Some killers, sick of the crimes they have committed, may send a note to the police confessing to the crimes. Some may call a local newspaper to ask for help. But eventually the fantasies begin again, and the uncontrollable urge to murder overtakes the killer. Once again, the killing phases begin.

Jeffrey Dahmer, who killed 18 victims over a 13-year period, at his arraignment on four counts of murder, July 25, 1991. According to psychologist Joel Norris, serial killers go through a period of deep depression following each murder. The fact remains, however, that few turn themselves in, and almost all will go on killing until stopped by the police.

HUNTING HUMANS: LAW ENFORCEMENT AND THE SERIAL KILLER

The official search for a killer begins at the moment a body is found—or sooner, if a victim disappears under suspicious circumstances. Detectives collect evidence from the crime scene and interview witnesses, if there are any. A medical examiner inspects the body for forensic evidence, such as hair, blood, or fiber samples, and performs an autopsy to establish the cause and time of death and the type of weapons used.

If the victim's identity is known, family members, friends, and associates are interviewed in an attempt to discover possible motives and to reconstruct the victim's movements during the last hours of his or her life.

The largest percentage of murders are committed by

Investigators examine the body of a woman found near New York's Kennedy Airport. Frequently, the bodies of serial murder victims lie undiscovered for long periods, during which forensic evidence degrades. This is but one of the factors that complicates the hunt for serial killers.

57

people who knew the victim and who aren't skilled at killing. Often these are crimes of passion and the perpetrators are so emotionally overwrought that they leave important clues and witnesses at the crime scene. When police question them closely, these killers are apt to betray their guilt through inconsistencies in their stories.

Even when the murder was well planned and obvious clues are absent, police always check lovers, family members, and associates, and frequently a compelling motive—money, jealousy, revenge—casts suspicion on a person. With a motive established, police can dig for any loose ends the killer has overlooked.

And even in felony murder cases—in which the murder was committed as a secondary act and the killer didn't know the victim—solving the first crime usually solves the murder case. For example, if a burglar kills the owner of a house he is robbing, the clues that lead police to the burglar also lead them to the murderer. In these kinds of investigations, which involve professional criminals, informants can be very useful by leading police to stolen goods or providing the names of people involved. Many felony murders are drug related, and once again, informants and street dealers can often shed light on what happened.

In cases of contract murder—murder for hire and mob-related murder—the killers are skilled at what they do. They know how to cover their tracks and fade into the background. Nevertheless, the motives for the murder are generally apparent, and often the police can follow the trail from the person who hired the killer to the person who actually committed the murder.

The key in all these cases is that police can establish a clear relationship between the killer and the victim. There is a logical motive for the slaying, even if it isn't always readily apparent.

The serial murderer is an entirely different criminal. The only connection he has with his victims is in his

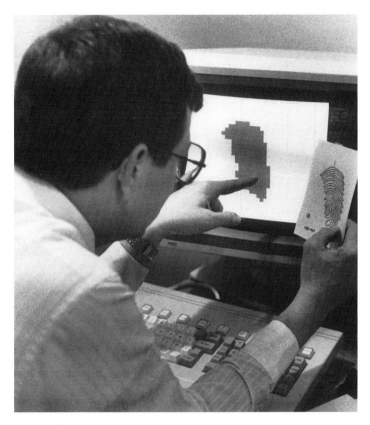

Despite recent technological advances such as DNA testing and automated fingerprint identification (shown here), the solution rate for homicides in the United States has declined significantly in the last three decades. The reason: traditional investigative and forensic techniques often prove useless in solving "stranger homicides," which now account for a sizable proportion of the murders in this country.

mind. Plus, he is likely to be quite skilled at what he does, having rehearsed the actual murder over and over again. If he is an organized killer, he knows how to select victims he can handle, and after he has killed, he'll hide the body. As a result, the victim may be missing for months or even years before the body is discovered, and by the time police begin investigating the crime, critical evidence has been obliterated. In addition, as previously discussed, organized serial murderers frequently abduct, kill, and dispose of their victims in different locations, which further obscures the relationship between killer and victim and complicates the task of evidence collection.

Only 30 years ago, police in the United States were solving about 90 percent of homicide cases within a year. But that rate has declined significantly. In 1995,

for example, 35 percent of homicides went unsolved, according to the FBI's Uniform Crime Report. The principal reason, experts say, is that up to 10,000 murders each year are now "stranger homicides" (in which the victim and the killer didn't know each other) or killings in which police can discern no connection between victim and killer. Serial murder falls squarely

The Green River near Seattle, Washington. It was here that a serial killer—or, some authorities believe, several serial killers— dumped the bodies of 49 victims. Despite the efforts of a massive task force, the Green River Killer was never caught.

into this category.

As the scope of the serial murder problem became evident in the 1970s and early 1980s, law enforcement officials, faced with the realization that traditional investigative methods weren't working, scrambled to develop new responses. One of these was an increased use of the special task force.

Albert DeSalvo (at right) was identified as the notorious Boston Strangler only after a fellow inmate at a mental institution reported his suspicions. A profile of the Strangler prepared by a distinguished group of psychiatrists and psychologists had given police a wildly inaccurate picture of the man they were looking for.

The task force consists of detectives who are assigned full time to a particular investigation and who perform specific tasks: interviewing witnesses, fanning out to gather information from people who live near the crime scene or who knew the victim, responding to tips phoned in to a special hot line, gathering information from other jurisdictions, working with the FBI or other federal authorities, securing crime scenes, working with forensics specialists. Essentially, the special task force is designed to ensure that all possible avenues of investigation are pursued, a luxury that regular homicide units don't always have because of a lack of investigators or other resources.

Often the results of such intensive police work more than justify the high cost. David Berkowitz, for example, was caught only after a task force followed a seemingly unpromising lead to the killer. A witness recalled seeing a car with a parking ticket on it near one of the murder scenes, and the task force checked the records of all parking tickets issued in the area that night, tracing one to a car registered to Berkowitz. The serial killer was arrested before he could carry out his plan to shoot up a crowded nightclub, an assault that could well have cost scores of lives.

Perhaps the most important weapon the police have in fighting a serial murderer is the behavioral profile. Profiling is based on the premise that an astute observer expert in criminal behavior can, from evidence found at the crime scene—such as where the body was left, who the victim was, and what condition the body was in—infer a great deal about who the offender was.

Today most of the criminal profiling for serial murder cases is done by specially trained agents at the FBI. But profiling got its start when, in the mid-1950s, New York City police enlisted the help of a psychiatrist in their investigation into a string of bombings. After studying photographs of the crime scenes and analyzing letters the perpetrator had sent to newspapers, Dr. James A. Brussel developed a remarkably detailed profile of the man known as the Mad Bomber. Police would find the bomber, Brussel said, living in a city in Connecticut. He would be foreign-born, probably of Eastern European descent. He would be in his forties, a Roman Catholic, heavy-set, and single. He hated his father and loved his mother obsessively (Brussel made this last inference from the way the bomber's *w*'s resembled breasts). And when taken into custody, Brussel predicted, the bomber would be wearing a buttoned, double-breasted suit. Sure enough, when the police finally arrested George Metesky, they found that he resembled

Brussel's profile of the Mad Bomber in nearly every respect—down to the buttoned, double-breasted suit.

While the remarkable accuracy of Brussel's profile seemed to presage a new era in crime solving, other early profiles weren't as successful. In the 1960s, for example, a group of distinguished psychiatrists and psychologists—including Dr. Brussel—drew up a behavioral profile of the Boston Strangler. The profile didn't resemble the actual killer, Albert DeSalvo, and many law enforcement professionals grew skeptical of the merits of behavioral profiling.

In the early 1970s profiling was done occasionally and informally at the FBI's Behavioral Science Unit in Quantico, Virginia. At the time, the unit consisted of a handful of special agents whose primary responsibility was teaching courses on hostage negotiations to law enforcement professionals. At the request of local police departments, several of the agents would generate profiles, drawing heavily on anecdotal evidence and their own experiences with cases that seemed similar.

Profiling took a quantum leap forward when, in the late 1970s, Robert Ressler and his associates at the Behavioral Science Unit began interviewing incarcerated murderers. The new insights they gained into the minds and motivations of serial killers would prove invaluable. And Ressler and his colleagues were able to verify some beliefs long held by police. They discovered, for example, that many murderers do, indeed, return to the scene of their crimes—not out of a sense of guilt, as had been assumed, but rather to relive the excitement of their act. As a result of the rigorous research Ressler's group undertook, for the first time assumptions about serial killers could be checked, patterns identified, and sound, real-world behavioral science brought to bear in developing consistently accurate profiles.

Many people have misperceptions about the role of behavioral profiles, profilers, and the FBI in hunting serial killers. Movies such as *The Silence of the Lambs* and TV series such as *Profiler* add to the confusion. First of all, profilers don't pursue serial killers themselves; local police do that. At their discretion, the local police may consult the FBI's experts, frequently by sending photos of crime scenes and other evidence to Quantico. From a careful analysis of this evidence, combined with what they know about the behavior of serial killers and the experience they've had in evaluating other crime scenes, the FBI experts will draw up a profile detailing characteristics of the probable offender. This profile is then sent back to the police department that requested it.

Although profiles can be quite detailed, they do *not* point police to the one person who could have committed a given murder or set of murders. Rather, they enable police to rule out large segments of the population and to focus on a relatively small number of promising suspects. Often, after receiving a profile, the police will realize that they've already interviewed the killer, or the profile will confirm that the person they consider the prime suspect is indeed the likely killer.

Much of the information that goes into a profile is based upon known characteristics of serial murderers. For example, most serial killers are white men and most are between the ages of 25 and 35. Furthermore, serial murder is usually an intraracial crime: if the victims are white, the killer is most likely white; if the victims are

Actor Anthony Hopkins as serial killer/psychiatrist Dr. Hannibal Lecter in The Silence of the Lambs. Though it garnered critical praise, the 1991 film presented a somewhat distorted view of the FBI's role in catching serial murderers.

The FBI considers Aileen Wuornos (above), who confessed to shooting seven men on Florida interstates, the first documented female serial killer. When confronted with a clear case of serial murder, an FBI profiler will assume the killer is male.

black, the killer is probably black. There are, of course, exceptions. Carlton Gary, the Columbus Stocking Strangler, was black, but his victims were all elderly white women.

By looking at the crime scene, a profiler can usually determine whether the police are dealing with an organized or a disorganized offender. Sometimes individual clues are misleading, so the whole crime scene must be viewed in context. For example, a body found in plain view soon after a murder took place ordinarily represents the work of a disorganized killer. But though they were actually highly organized, Kenneth Bianchi and Angelo Buono Jr., two sadistic cousins who together committed San Francisco's Hillside Strangler murders in the late 1970s, nevertheless dumped the bodies of their victims along the sides of roads where they couldn't be missed. This most likely was intended as a challenge to the police. Once the category of offender has been established, the known characteristics of that type can help in making further assumptions about the particular killer.

The rest of profiling largely boils down to insight and the ability to make logical inferences. Perhaps the best way to understand the process is to look at an actual case.

Around six o'clock one Sunday morning in September 1983, a 13-year-old boy from Bellevue, Nebraska, a suburb of Omaha, disappeared after delivering the first three newspapers on his paper route. His bike and the remaining newspapers were found near the fourth house on his route. No signs of a struggle were apparent. The missing child was white, 5'2", and 100 pounds.

Two days later, the boy's body, clad only in underpants, was found alongside a little-traveled gravel road about four miles from where his bike had been left. Though the body was in tall weeds, it was still partially visible from the road. The boy's arms and legs were tied behind his back with rope, and surgical tape covered his mouth and also bound his hands and feet. The back of his neck had been slashed, he had been stabbed repeatedly in the chest and back, slices of flesh had been removed from a shoulder and the inside of one leg, and a crisscross pattern had been carved into a calf, apparently after the boy was dead. There were no indications of sexual assault. The medical examiner's report indicated that the boy had been alive a day after the abduction and that the body had been moved after the murder. The absence of rope abrasions suggested that for some time after the abduction the boy wasn't tied up and may not have been harshly treated.

In *Whoever Fights Monsters*, Robert Ressler describes how this evidence formed the basis for his first profile of the Bellevue murderer. The killer, Ressler predicted, was a white male in his late teens or early twenties, and this was probably his first murder. Physically, he might be small or weak. He was from the local area, and he may have known the victim. Though of average intelligence, he had no more than a high school education. He lived alone or with parents who didn't keep close tabs on him, was single, and had never had sex with a consenting peer. He frequently read pornography. In his adolescence, he'd probably performed bizarre experiments on animals or attempted to force sex on younger children. He'd recently experienced a stressful event, such as a breakup with a girlfriend or family troubles, and he may have been absent from his job in the days preceding and following the abduction and murder.

How had Ressler arrived at these conclusions? First of all, he could be sure that the killer was a white male because the wounds on the victim's body, particularly the mutilation, suggested a sexual homicide, and serial killers are, in his view, invariably male and usually white. (The fact that the victim was in his undershorts might also have pointed to a sexual dimension to the crime, or it might simply have indicated an attempt by the killer to discourage the boy from trying to run away.) In addition, serial killers rarely choose victims of a different race, and since the boy was white, the killer was most likely white. Plus, the abduction had taken place in a white neighborhood, where someone of a different race would have stood out.

The killer's probable age—late teens to early twenties—and the belief that this was his first murder were based on the location and condition of the body. The wounds suggested a somewhat tentative killer: the neck slash seemed to have been an unsuccessful attempt at decapitation—perhaps the killer hadn't realized how difficult that would be—and the crisscross pattern on the calf, though indicative of ritual, wasn't very clear, another sign that the killer hadn't done this before. Then there was the location. The body was dumped near a road, where the killer could have been spotted by a passing car. An older, more experienced murderer wouldn't have taken that chance.

Ressler believed that the killer was small and not particularly strong because though there was an attempt to conceal the body in tall grass, the site was close to the road. A large or strong killer, even if he were inexperienced, would probably have carried the body further from the road to better hide it.

The fact that the killer dumped the body off a remote road not far from the abduction site and that

the victim was probably alive, and maybe not even tied up, for about a day after the abduction, suggested that the killer was from the area. He knew the local roads, it seemed, plus he must have had a house nearby, or at least known of someplace where he and the victim could have been together without being noticed. And the fact that there was apparently no struggle at the abduction scene indicated that the victim may have known the killer at least casually, another reason to believe he was a local.

Although the crime showed a degree of planning—the boy was abducted without anyone noticing, and the killer had rope and tape handy to restrain him, for example—several contingencies had been unanticipated. This was why Ressler felt that the killer was only of

Wayne Williams (center, with open collar), the accused Atlanta Child Killer, leaves court after a day of testimony in his murder trial. Williams was caught after an FBI profiler predicted that the serial murderer who was targeting black youths would begin dumping bodies in a river. A police surveillance team spotted Williams's car stopping on a bridge at night and heard a loud splash, and a body was later recovered downriver.

average intelligence and had at most a high school education. A college-educated or more intelligent killer would have foreseen that disposing of the body could be difficult, and he would have addressed that problem in planning the murder, Ressler felt.

The victim had been abducted around 6:00 A.M. on a Sunday and had been alive and in the company of the killer the rest of the day. Several inferences could be drawn from these facts. One is that the killer had no one to whom he was responsible—a spouse, a live-in partner, parents—who presumably would have noted his absence or seen the victim. Ressler found further evidence that the killer was single from the fact that the victim hadn't been sexually assaulted. In most cases in which mutilation is present but there is no sexual assault, the killer hasn't had any consensual sexual experiences and often hasn't had any sexual experiences at all.

But the mutilation indicated that the killer had strong, deviant sexual fantasies, and such fantasies typically evolve over the course of many years. In all likelihood the fantasies would have been fueled by pornography and would have manifested themselves in earlier incidents such as the killing of small animals or attempted sexual assaults on younger children.

With organized killers—and this murderer showed many of the hallmarks of one—a stressful event usually precipitates the first murder. Having already concluded that this was the killer's first murder, Ressler could predict with a reasonable degree of confidence that the killer had recently encountered job or interpersonal troubles or some other stressful situation. And he may well have missed a few days of work before and after the murder—many serial killers do, as this is for them an especially important time in their ritual.

A few months after the first murder, in December of 1983, another 13-year-old boy was abducted near Omaha. Standing slightly over five feet tall and weigh-

ing 85 pounds, this child, whose father worked at the Offutt Air Force Base, had been walking to school at 8:30 A.M. when witnesses saw him get into a car driven by a white male. His body was found three days later in a wooded area about five miles away. Like the first victim, he had been stabbed and was wearing only underpants; the rest of his clothes were in a neat pile near the body. Once again, no sexual assault had occurred. This time, however, the postmortem mutilation was more extensive; some of the cuts were over bite marks. And the victim had been killed where the body was found: two sets of footprints in the snow led into the woods; only one led out.

Based on evidence from the new murder, Ressler revised his profile of the killer. He now concluded that

Serial murderers sometimes work in pairs. Such was the case with Kenneth Bianchi (shown here testifying at a pretrial hearing) and his cousin Angelo Buono Jr., who together committed the Hillside Strangler murders.

the murderer was in his twenties rather than his late teens. This was based on the increased level of planning involved in the more recent crime: the killer had made the victim march into the woods with him, had gotten him to strip to his underpants, and had killed him where he wouldn't have to worry about moving the body. This also convinced Ressler that he'd been right about the killer's small stature. He was probably not much bigger than his victims.

The site chosen for the second killing showed a familiarity with the region that confirmed Ressler's earlier belief that the murderer lived nearby. He now felt that the killer worked at the Offutt Air Force Base, where the family of the more recent victim lived. And, based on his estimation of the killer's education and intelligence, he stated that the killer was probably a low-ranking airman—a maintenance man or mechanic in all likelihood.

The cuts over the bite marks on the second victim cast light on the reason the killer had sliced flesh from the first victim's shoulder and leg: he was attempting to make it impossible for investigators to identify him through the pattern of his bite. From this Ressler concluded that the killer read detective and police magazines, where such identification techniques are frequently discussed.

The fact that the murder of the second victim had taken place in the middle of the woods yet the killer had still stripped the boy to his undershorts "stood out boldly," Ressler felt, "as a sexual matter, not as a control action."

He might be attempting to deny it, but the killer was a homosexual—although, as further confirmed by the absence of sexual assault in the second case, he had little or no sexual experience. What the killings represented, Ressler concluded, "was a killer's anger at himself, expressed as homicidal rage toward victims who in his mind mirrored the boy he had been at their age."

Ressler's profile included one last piece of information, and it was chilling: the killer would work with young boys—as a Boy Scouts leader, as a Little League coach, or in some similar capacity. This prediction was based on the ease with which he had abducted the boys.

Armed with the profile, the local police launched an intensive effort to catch the killer before he struck again. Fortunately, they succeeded. John Joseph Joubert IV was picked up at his quarters on Offutt Air Force Base, where investigators found a hunting knife, rope, and detective magazines. Joubert matched the profile of the killer quite well. He was 21 years old, 5'6" and slightly built, and he worked as a radar technician doing maintenance. He was an assistant scoutmaster of a local Boy Scouts troop.

Joubert had had violent fantasies since age six or seven, when he fantasized about strangling and eating a baby-sitter. As he grew older, the content of his fantasies shifted from killing girls to killing boys. At the age of 13, the same age as his victims, Joubert experienced what for him was the traumatic loss of a friend. He returned from a summer vacation to find that the boy's family had moved away, and Joubert's mother refused to help her son locate his friend so that he could reestablish contact. Soon afterward, Joubert drove a pencil into the back of a young girl as he rode past her on his bike. Like his first victim at Bellevue, the 13-year-old John Joubert had a morning paper route.

After a high school career in which he was tormented by classmates as a suspected homosexual, Joubert decided to attend college but dropped out after a year. He joined the air force and went through basic training in Texas, where he met and became close to another young airman. When both were assigned to Offutt, they decided to be roommates. But other airmen on the base soon began insinuating that the two were lovers, and Joubert's roommate moved out. That was the precrime stress that Ressler had predicted in his

In many cases, missing persons are accounted for only after a captured serial murderer leads authorities to a burial site. Here forensics experts scour the grounds of a house formerly occupied by serial killer Jeffrey Dahmer. They are looking for any trace of the remains of a person missing for 13 years.

profile: about a week after his roommate left, Joubert abducted and murdered the paperboy.

In some cases, a psychological profile will not only give police a picture of a serial killer but will also suggest strategies for catching him. For example, a profile might predict that a given killer will return to the site of a crime or visit the graves of his victims, in which case police can stake out those places. In the case of the Atlanta child murders of 1979 to 1981, a profiler believed that, after the newspapers had reported the recovery of fiber evidence from several victims, the killer would begin dumping bodies in a river. Wayne Williams, eventually convicted of two of the killings and presumed responsible for a dozen more, came under suspicion after his car stopped on a bridge one night and an officer stationed below on the banks of the river heard a large splash. A body was later recovered downstream.

A profile can also give police guidance on how to interrogate serial murder suspects. For example, certain killers are likely to pass a lie-detector test, and administering one will only increase their confidence. Some killers will tend to confess if the interrogator intimates that the victim was partly responsible for his or her fate; others will get rattled if the police maintain constant pressure. With still other killers, feigning incompetence leads to a full confession as the killer demonstrates what he considers his superiority to the police.

Another tool that law enforcement has brought to bear on the problem of catching serial killers is nationwide information sharing. In the past, many serial murder investigations were crippled by the problem of multiple police jurisdictions. Police departments in different parts of a state—or even different parts of the country—would be investigating murders committed by the same person, but they had no way of knowing this and therefore no way of sharing information that might prove useful. Pierce Brooks, a Los Angeles Police Department homicide detective, ran into this problem in the 1950s while investigating a series of rapes and murders that he believed were related.

With no other way to find out whether neighboring jurisdictions had similar unsolved crimes, Brooks resorted to scanning local newspapers and police files. Though he eventually caught the killer, he realized that there was a tremendous need for a more efficient way of obtaining information from other jurisdictions. He dreamed of a statewide computer system on which police would record the details of their unsolved homicides and to which they could turn if they wanted to check for similar crimes in other jurisdictions. At the time, however, computer technology wasn't advanced or cheap enough to make this feasible.

Bob Keppel was another cop who recognized the need for interjurisdictional information sharing. Keppel, a homicide investigator in Seattle, Washington, spent years trying to solve the slayings of some 35 female college students.

A woman named Elizabeth Kendall told Seattle police that she suspected her former fiancé, Ted Bundy, but the police investigated and cleared Bundy on at least two separate occasions. Only after Kendall informed them of a similar pattern of crimes taking place in the Salt Lake City area, where Bundy had relocated, did they reopen the inquiry.

Eventually Keppel was able to identify Bundy as the prime suspect in the Seattle area's unsolved murder cases. By this time, though, Bundy had been convicted of an attempted kidnapping in Utah, had escaped while awaiting trial for murder in Colorado, and had fled to Florida. After Elizabeth Kendall read a news item about two rape-murders in a sorority house on the Tallahassee campus of Florida State University, she notified the FBI that she thought the murderer might be Ted Bundy, but they didn't give her suspicions much credence until Bundy was arrested in Florida for the rape and murder of a 12-year-old girl.

Keppel met Pierce Brooks when the two were hired as consultants to the Atlanta Police Department for the child murder case of 1979 to 1981. Their discussions renewed Brooks's dream of a computer database of unsolved homicides.

That dream was realized in the mid-1980s, when the Violent Criminal Apprehension Program (VICAP) was established under the auspices of the FBI's National Center for the Analysis of Violent Crime. Brooks served as VICAP's first director.

The VICAP process begins with a detailed form that local police fill out when they have an unsolved violent crime in their jurisdiction. The form includes straightforward information, such as where and when the crime occurred, as well as details of the forensic evidence and a description of the perpetrator's modus operandi, or MO (the way he or she went about committing the crime). The police then submit the form to the FBI, where the information is entered into the VICAP database.

Local police, in turn, can access the database to learn whether, for example, a crime they are investigating bears an MO similar to that of crimes committed elsewhere, whether a similar crime was committed elsewhere while a suspect in their case was in that area, or whether a weapon they've confiscated from a suspect is linked to other crimes. In this way, VICAP has proven a valuable tool not only in the fight against serial killers, but in the investigation of all violent crime as well.

A GROWING MENACE?

During the mid-1980s, concern about serial murderers bordered on hysteria as news accounts documented a proliferation of these killers and described in detail their heinous crimes. While it is undeniable that serial killers are among society's most dangerous individuals, the real threat serial murder poses should not be overstated. In a nation of more than 250 million people, the FBI estimates that around 500 serial killers are at large and unidentified. Thankfully, serial murder is still rare.

That said, given the terrible suffering they inflict, a rate of even one serial killer per half-million citizens seems unacceptably high. Plus, the number of serial killers is increasing. Robert Ressler believes that society has always been—and will always be—plagued by a small, relatively unchanging percentage of disorganized killers whose actions are the result of their psychotic loss of touch with reality. But fueling the recent rise in serial murders, he says, is an increase in the number of

The havoc wreaked by a serial killer: still a rare sight, but becoming less so.

organized killers, who are in touch with reality yet choose to commit their crimes nonetheless.

Various factors might explain this phenomenon. First of all, ours is a mobile, impersonal society. People move freely from place to place, often without establishing deep ties to the community. This makes serial murder easier to get away with. Secondly, images of violence and sexuality, the stuff of a serial killer's fantasies, pervade the media. Finally—and perhaps most important of all—there is plenty of real violence and sexual abuse in our culture. And as we have seen, a strong link exists between childhood abuse and later serial murder.

What, then, can society do about the growing menace of serial killers? The problem, which is arguably exacerbated by the very nature of our culture, defies easy solutions. On the law enforcement front, steps typically proposed to combat crime in general—more police on the streets or tougher sentencing, for example—won't have an impact because serial killers don't share the motivations of other criminals. The best hope lies with advanced investigative techniques and effective collaboration between local and national law enforcement agencies, as manifested by programs like the FBI's profiling unit and VICAP. But experts acknowledge that these efforts barely keep pace with the growing problem.

Turning the corner on the problem—preventing potential serial killers from becoming actual serial killers—would require a massive, coordinated effort by law enforcement and legal, medical, mental-health, and social-service institutions. To be successful, such an effort would have to address social problems like dysfunctional parenting and child abuse, problems that have thus far proven intractable. In addition, a greater awareness of the warning signs of serial murder would have to be cultivated among medical and mental-health professionals, and these professionals would need the authority to intervene when such signs were

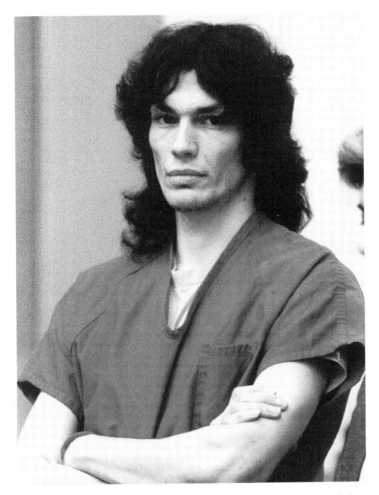

Serial killers like Richard Ramirez, "the Night Stalker" of Los Angeles, are certain to plague our society for the foreseeable future.

present. And courts would have to be cognizant of the patterns of escalating violence and antisocial behavior, particularly sexually deviant behavior, that characterize those who go on to become serial killers—and would perhaps have to incarcerate certain young sex offenders indefinitely.

Realistically, none of this is likely to happen. For the foreseeable future, then, we can be sure that living among us and waiting for an opportunity to strike will be a small but growing number of twisted people who strive to make their nightmarish fantasies real.

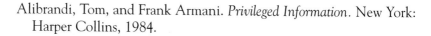

Alibrandi, Tom, and Frank Armani. *Privileged Information*. New York: Harper Collins, 1984.

Anderson, Chris, and Sharon McGehee. *Bodies of Evidence*. New York: Lyle Stuart, 1991.

Bledsoe, Jerry. *Bitter Blood*. New York: E. P. Dutton, 1988.

Brussel, James A. *Casebook of a Crime Psychiatrist*. New York: Bernard Geis, 1968.

Cahill, Tim. *Buried Dreams*. New York: Bantam, 1985.

Cox, Mike. *The Confessions of Henry Lee Lucas*. New York: Ivy, 1991.

Crockett, Art. *Serial Murderers*. New York: Pinnacle, 1990.

Douglas, John, and Mark Olshaker. *Mind Hunter: Inside the FBI's Elite Serial Crime Unit*. New York: Pocket Books, 1995.

Gelb, Barbara. *On the Track of Murder*. New York: William Morrow, 1975.

Green, Jonathon. *The Greatest Criminals of All Time*. New York: Stein & Day, 1982.

Hickey, Eric. *Serial Murderers and Their Victims*. 2nd ed. Belmont, Calif.: Wadsworth Publishing Co., 1997.

Holmes, Ronald, and James De Burger. *Serial Murder*. Newbury Park, Calif.: Sage, 1988.

Keppel, Robert D. *Serial Murder: Future Implications for Police Investigations*. Cincinnati: Anderson Publishing Co., 1989.

Leyton, Elliott. *Compulsive Killers*. New York: New York University Press, 1986.

Magid, Ken, and Carole A. McKelvey. *High Risk: Children Without a Conscience*. New York: Bantam, 1987.

Michaud, Stephen, and Hugh Aynesworth. *The Only Living Witness*. New York: Simon and Schuster, 1983.

Nash, Jay Robert. *Bloodletters and Badmen*. New York: Evans, 1973.

Newton, Michael. *Hunting Humans*. Port Townsend, Wash.: Loompanics, 1990.

Norris, Joel. *Serial Killers: The Growing Menace*. New York: Doubleday, 1988.

Pettit, Mark. *A Need to Kill*. New York: Ivy Books, 1990.

Ressler, Robert K., and Tom Shachtman. *Whoever Fights Monsters*. New York: St. Martin's Press, 1992.

Ressler, Robert K., Ann W. Burgess, and John E. Douglas. *Sexual Homicide: Patterns and Motives*. Lexington, Mass.: Lexington Books, 1988.

Rule, Ann. *Lust Killer*. New York: New American Library, 1983.

Schechter, Harold. *Deviant: The Shocking True Story of the Original "Psycho."* New York: Pocket Books, 1989.

U.S. Judiciary Committee. *Serial Murders: Hearing on Patterns of Murders Committed by One Person, in Large Numbers with No Apparent Rhyme, Reason, or Motivation*. Washington, D.C.: U.S. Government Printing Office, 1984.

Van Hoffmann, Eric. *A Venom in the Blood*. New York: Donald I. Fine, 1990.

Yallop, David. *Deliver Us from Evil*. New York: Coward, McCann, 1982.

Index

Picture Credits

Writer ROBERT W. DOLAN is a former New York City police officer.

AUSTIN SARAT is William Nelson Cromwell Professor of Jurisprudence & Political Science at Amherst College, where he also chairs the Department of Law, Jurisprudence and Social Thought. Professor Sarat is the author or editor of 23 books and numerous scholarly articles. Among his books are *Law's Violence*, *Sitting in Judgment: Sentencing the White Collar Criminal*, and *Justice and Injustice in Law and Legal Theory*. He has received many academic awards and held several prestigious fellowships. In addition, he is a nationally recognized teacher and educator whose teaching has been featured in the *New York Times*, on the *Today* show, and on National Public Radio's *Fresh Air*.